THE

BLOOM

Copyright © 2025 by GraceyBeInspired
All rights reserved. No part of this publication may be reproduced, distributed, or transmitted in any form or by any means, including photocopying, recording, or other electronic or mechanical methods, without the prior written permission of the publisher, except in the case of brief quotations embodied in critical reviews and certain other noncommercial uses permitted by copyright law.

Limit of Liability / Disclaimer of Warranty
The information in this book is provided "as is," with no guarantees of completeness, accuracy, usefulness, or timeliness. While the author has made every effort to ensure the information contained in *The Bloom* is accurate and based on personal experience, reflection, and research, neither the author nor the publisher shall be held liable for any loss, damage, or disruption caused by reliance on any content or information contained within.

This book is not intended to serve as professional advice in areas such as medical, legal, therapeutic, or psychological services. Readers are encouraged to seek guidance from qualified professionals where appropriate. The use of this book and its contents is at the reader's own discretion and risk

For permission requests, write to the publisher at:
Kindle Direct Publishing

ISBN: [979-8-89778-302-1]
Cover design by: [Joshua Alfred (Cedar Creatives) +2347085320668]
Edited by: [Gracey Agbana Babatunde]
Printed in [UK]
First Edition

"Everything we face in life carries a purpose - Let your scares be the ink that writes your story of impact"

Gracey Be Inspired

THE FOREWORD

I have personally known Gracey and watched her navigate many different seasons filled with deep pain and mountain top joy, in the 15 years since we met. I watched her struggle to get pregnant and was there in the labour ward as she delivered her beautiful first daughter Alexis. I've watched her lead a choir and sing so beautifully and heard her hysterical cries when she was plunged into the next valley of life. However, through it all she has never denied her faith in a loving and faithful God, who hears, restores, renews and rejuvenates.

The Bloom is an extraordinary and poignant memoir that traces the harrowing journey of a woman who has triumphed over unimaginable trials. Written with raw emotion and an unflinching honesty, this book explores the profound effects of sexual abuse by a family member, the betrayal by a trusted medical professional, and the devastating disillusionment of a failed marriage. Yet, amid these hardships, the author Gracey reveals a story of unwavering strength, resilience, and the eventual finding of peace and happiness in a second marriage to a loving and supportive man.

The author's ability to craft her story by using a fictional character called Tanwa, has been written with such grace, despite the painful circumstances she has endured, is nothing short of inspiring. Gracey does not shy away from the painful details of her past, but instead, uses them to demonstrate how courage and resilience can light the path toward healing. What stands out the most is her determination not to let these abuses define her. Through the betrayal of a trusted family member and then the duplicity and shocking behaviour of a 'professional doctor' Gracey continually finds a way to persevere, heal, and rise above the pain.

One of the most moving aspects of the book is her recounting of her tumultuous marriage, which became a symbol of broken trust and heartache. Betrayed by a husband who failed to recognize her emotional and physical trauma, she bravely navigates the storm of separation and divorce. Though the emotional scars are deep, the strength it takes to walk away from this relationship is a testament to her courage. The journey of the discovery of true Godly identity that follows her divorce is a powerful reminder that true healing can only begin when we embrace our own worth.

Through all the adversity, the author ultimately finds love again in a wonderful man, who becomes her partner in the truest sense of the word. This new chapter of her story is filled with hope and renewal, proving that it's never too late to find happiness after hardship. Her remarriage represents not just the possibility of a new life, but also the healing of old wounds.

Throughout the book there are explanations and information given that help readers of abuse recognise different areas and facets of destructive and toxic relationships. Gracey offers hope to her readers in that their painful, horrific past does not have to define the narrative of their future life and happiness.

This book is a profound exploration of human resilience and the ability to overcome even the darkest of circumstances. It is a beacon of hope for anyone who has experienced abuse, betrayal, or loss, and a reminder that with Godly courage, self-love, and perseverance, it is possible to reclaim one's life and joy again.

The Bloom is not just a memoir but a powerful message of empowerment. Gracey invites readers to reflect on their own strength and resilience and encourages them to believe in the transformative power of self-acceptance and love. This is a must-read for anyone seeking inspiration.

Elizabeth Duthie.

TABLE OF CONTENTS

1. THE BLOOM

2. HEALING CHAPTER

3. SELF ESTEEM CHAPTER

4. WAITING CHAPTER

5. GRIEF CHAPTER

6. DON'T BLAME YOU CHAPTER

7. STANDING IN LOVE CHAPTER

8. CHANGED STORY CHAPTER

THE BLOOM

"The lion has fallen," she thought, her eyes fixed on her father's lifeless body in a white coffin. He had always been a towering figure in her life but not the kind of hero others saw. To Tanwa, he was a man of rage, the source of her childhood fears. As cousins and distant relatives wailed around him, mourning the loss of a man they revered, she felt a hollow detachment.

She searched within herself for grief but found nothing—only a numbness that came from years of scars, now sealed and silenced perpetually.

"The lion has fallen," Tanwa thought, but her eyes were drawn away from the white coffin and toward her mother's sealed grave, just a few feet away.

Her mother had passed over a decade ago, yet the pain of that loss still felt fresh, like an open wound. Starring at the grave, her chest tightened as she remembered the gentleness and warmth that was taken from her long ago.

While others wept for her father, she felt the old grief of losing the one person who had truly shown her the kind of love she understood. That pain was real, unlike the emptiness she felt for the man in the coffin.

Mother... fondly called MoMo, had a strength that allowed her to keep a positive outlook, even when things were difficult. Smiling through the hardships, especially in situations where she might have felt stuck or unfulfilled, speaks to resilience and maybe a sense of duty. MoMo kept up appearances for the sake of those she loved or because she felt like she didn't have other options. She didn't fully realise or believe in the possibility of a different life for herself... So, MoMo stayed consistent—even to her dying day—a true example of the marriage vows "till death do us part."

Looking back now, it's heartbreakingly clear- MoMo had no options. Her childhood was a field of thorns sown with rejection, watered with silence and starved of dreams. No bright future was ever painted before her. No one told her she could become more. All she saw were shadows. All she heard was endure.

So, she was told she was betrothed –handed over to a man she barely knew-there was no room for rebellion. No space to question. No whisper of "what if".

This was the path. Not chosen but carved by hand she couldn't fight. And so, she walked.

In her world, being a good wife was not about joy, it was about survival, it was loyalty, respect...... Silence. It was folding pain into the corners of her soul and wearing a strong face even as her heart broke in private.

She didn't know any other way. There was no education to give her a language for her pain, no exposure to teach her that love shouldn't roar like a lion and leave scars like claws.

And so, even when the man she married growled instead of speaking. Even when his presence felt more like a cage than a covering...Even when he trampled on the girl who once dared to dream...There was only one option...Stay...Not because she loved it, but because the world told her she had no choice. And she did. Every day.... Every year.... She stayed because in her story, strength didn't look like escape, it looked like surviving where others would have broken.

That makes a lot of sense, and it's understandable that her influence would have had a strong impact on her daughter Tanwa. Without other female mentors, it's natural to absorb not only her words and values but also her outlook and choices.

Observing her strength and perhaps her sacrifices closely—this experience created a deep imprint in Tanwa on how to approach life, sometimes shaping perspectives on relationships, self-worth, and the possibilities ahead.

It was both challenging and inspiring learning from MoMo while also sensing that there could have been different paths for her life.

That's so understandable. When real care or affection hasn't been a big part of our early experience, even small gestures can feel overwhelmingly meaningful. It can make us interpret gestures of love or kindness as something much bigger than they are, sometimes leading to relationships where the other person's intentions or level of commitment don't quite match our expectations.

This leads to staying in situations that feel fulfilling simply because they offered a level of care that was new — even if, in hindsight, those relationships might not have been what was truly needed.

Becoming aware of this pattern is such a powerful step, though, because it opens the door to seeing relationships more clearly and learning what genuine love, respect, and care look like.

You don't get joy without being open to pain!

Abuse can take many forms and recognising them is the first step toward prevention and, subsequently, healing. Here are the main types of abuses:

1. PHYSICAL ABUSE

This involves causing bodily harm through hitting, slapping, kicking, burning, or other forms of violence.

Furthermore, it may include threats of physical harm or withholding of basic needs like food and shelter.

Growing up in a place like Africa, where the line between discipline and physical abuse is often blurred, Tanwa did not escape the harsh realities that many children endure. What was labelled as "correction" often left deep emotional and physical imprints. It was a culture where obedience was demanded, sometimes through fear, and where a child's voice was rarely heard.

In the oppressive confines of their daily lives, Tanwa and her siblings learned early that every misstep incurred a harsh penalty. Their world was a prison where punishment was as relentless as it was brutal—from the searing lash of animal skin belts and the savage strikes of brittle tree stems and rods to the merciless deprivation of food. None escaped his tyranny, save for the lion himself.

At the first distant rumble of her father's car, the neighbourhood children scattered like leaves in a storm. His presence alone was enough to send shivers down spines—an unspoken warning etched into their young minds. The rigid discipline he had absorbed as a soldier clung to him like a second skin, transforming even the innocent into fugitives in their own streets. Yet, perhaps the most terrifying thing of all was that he had no idea just how fearsome he truly was.

Looking back now, she realises how much those experiences shaped her—both in pain and resilience. They teach you in silence, but they also stir a longing to break free, to heal, and to one day rewrite the narrative for those who would come after.

2. EMOTIONAL/PSYCHOLOGICAL ABUSE

This involves manipulation, intimidation, gaslighting, or verbal attacks that erode self-esteem and mental well-being.

Examples include constant criticism, humiliation, controlling behaviour, or isolation from loved ones.

Based on Tanwa's history of domestic abuse disguised as discipline, she continually found herself in situations where people took advantage of her gentle spirit. Unaware of any other way to live, she had learned from her mother to always maintain a calm demeanour—as the Bible teaches us to be as gentle as a dove—without realising that being as wise as a serpent is equally important. In her quest to please others, she repeatedly attracted relationships that were mentally abusive.

Marriage, Tanwa walked into it with hope, excitement, and a heart full of love. She believed in the fairytale, the prayers, the promises. But what she encountered was a different kind of pain — the kind that doesn't leave bruises on your skin, but on your soul. A kind that hides behind smiles in public and silence in private.

She was taken for granted — like her worth was invisible. Her sacrifices, her loyalty, her faithfulness — they were treated as expected, not appreciated.

And then came the betrayal even before Tanwa could get used to being married — quiet at first, like a shadow slipping through a crack in the door. He stepped outside the vows they once whispered to each other, and instead of remorse, he handed her the blame. His straying wore the mask of her supposed shortcomings. She was accused of being too much, or not enough — too loud, too quiet, too strong, too weak. The truth twisted into lies, and the lies dressed themselves as truth until she couldn't recognize herself in the mirror. The mind game was like poison in slow sips, blurring Tanwa's reality while she tried to hold on to the fragments of love she once believed in.

There's a unique kind of heartbreak that comes from being disrespected by the one who vowed to protect your heart. A betrayal that makes you shrink in silence because people expect you to endure. After all, you're married now. "Just pray more," they say. "Be patient," they add. But nobody tells you how to heal while carrying a bleeding heart.

Still, even in that darkness, Tanwa found light. She found the strength to stop covering wounds with makeup and smiles. She found her voice — the same voice she had lost trying to keep the peace. And she began to remember who she wanted to be as she had written down that seemed like fantasy: a woman full of purpose, power, and promise.

Tanwa believed she had found the man of her dreams, but even when it became painfully clear that he wasn't, she clung to the illusion. Marriage, instead of bringing her fulfilment, only deepened her struggles with self-esteem and loneliness.

After enduring years of betrayal and neglect, she finally summoned the courage to leave and embrace life as a single mother. Yet, the weight of her low self-worth pulled her back, leading her to plead for the restoration of a home that had long ceased to be one.

That night, she returned to the place she once called her marital home, hoping for a chance to mend what was broken. But his response to her unspoken plea shattered any lingering hope, marking the beginning of a new chapter -one where she would learn to lean on God, the only One who would never fail her.

Rejected once again, she walked away, her heart heavy with grief. She drove to the beach, sat in her car for over an hour, and wept—mourning not just the end of her marriage but the loss of over a decade of dreams that would never be.

Tanwa's experience speaks to the silent battles so many women face in toxic relationships, where self-worth becomes entangled in the idea of being chosen, even by someone who repeatedly rejects and disrespects them.

That moment at the beach, where she grieved the death of her marriage, felt like a turning point—a place where she finally faced the reality that she could no longer beg for love and respect that should have been freely given. It's heart-breaking, yet it also holds the potential for something beautiful: the realization that God's love is constant, and her healing began the moment she chose herself.

Over time, she discovered that acknowledging one's weaknesses and transforming them into strengths is one of the secrets to living a good life. Through her experiences and God's guidance, she learned that everything in life has a reason and a season. Some relationships are meant for a reason, some for a season, and some for a lifetime. Ultimately, her journey taught her to learn her lessons and move on, refusing to give herself reasons to remain in abusive relationships.

3. SEXUAL ABUSE

This involves every/any non-consensual sexual activity, including molestation, rape, coercion, or exploitation.

It can also involve inappropriate sexual comments, exposure, or forcing someone to participate in sexual acts.

Overcoming her sexual abuse was the most arduous challenge Tanwa had ever faced. Over the years, the trauma had become deeply ingrained, and the constant fear of being taken advantage of left her terrified and, paradoxically, drawn toward other abusive situations — one form of abuse seeming somehow lighter than another.

Tanwa had always believed there was a way out. After years of living under the weight of fear and silent screams, she clung to the whispers of hope she found in books and TV shows. The western world — it seemed like a place where pain could be spoken, where wounds could be heard, where healing wasn't a faraway dream but something real, reachable. She read about counselling — about the power of talking, of opening up, of being seen.

So, she took a bold step. She found a therapist. A man who wore calm like a coat, who spoke with the kind of gentleness that made you want to trust again. For the first time, she exhaled. She thought, *Maybe, just maybe, this is the beginning of my healing.*

But then... the unimaginable happened.

The very place that was meant to be her safe space — the very man who was supposed to guide her out of the shadows — became her new nightmare. He shattered what was left of her innocence, violating not just her body but the fragile trust she had barely begun to rebuild. Right there in the room where she was meant to unburden her soul, he became her second abuser. Another thief in disguise. Another betrayal wrapped in a smile.

The pain of what her father did was already a wound she carried like a second skin — but this? This was a new kind of agony. To have her trauma used as a doorway into deeper darkness. To have hope turn into horror.

She left that room broken all over again. Only now, the silence was heavier, the shame deeper, the healing even further away.

Repeated near-miss experiences with sexual abuse further eroded her self-esteem. When she attempted to share her fears, she was met with accusatory questions like, "Is there something about you that attracts these predators?" These hurtful responses only deepened her sense of blame and unworthiness, reinforcing the cycle that had so long controlled her life.

4. FINANCIAL/ECONOMIC ABUSE

This involves controlling or restricting a person's access to money or resources to maintain power over them.

Examples include preventing someone from working, stealing their earnings, or forcing them into financial dependency.

Tanwa had witnessed first-hand the silent chains that bound her mother—chains woven from financial control and an iron grip that extended far beyond money. Every glimmer of independence her mother reached for was swiftly dimmed by a man whose insecurities made him both her provider and her warden.

He stood like a barricade against her growth, dictating not just how she earned but how she spent.

Yet, despite his efforts to keep her caged, divine favour always found its way to her. But beneath that favour lay wounds—scars from a childhood stained with rejection and pain. Those scars whispered doubts into her thought pattern, which negatively affected her decisions; even though she was a very wise woman, she lingered in the shadows of her insecurities.

Still, God's mercy was relentless, guiding her even in her brokenness. "For I know the plans I have for you, declares the Lord, plans to prosper you and not to harm you, plans to give you a future and a hope." (Jeremiah 29:11)

Though life had tried to break her, grace held her together. And in time, she came to understand that "whom the Son sets free is free indeed." (John 8:36)

5. NEGLECT

This has to do with the failure to meet a person's basic needs, such as food, shelter, medical care, and emotional support.

It often affects children, the elderly, or individuals with disabilities.

Tanwa grew up knowing what it meant to be invisible. Not in the way of quiet children who shy away from attention but in the agonising way of a child whose presence was an afterthought. Neglect wasn't just an experience for her; it was the air she breathed.

Her father's eyes saw only what they could control, and his hands only reached for discipline, never for affection. Her mother, too weary from fighting battles she never won, had little left to pour into her children. So Tanwa, at an early stage in life, learned that love, at least the kind that nurtures and protects, was a luxury she would have to live without.

She found solace in silence, wrapping it around herself like a shield. Yet, the absence of care left a hunger in her soul, a gnawing emptiness that no amount of self-sufficiency could fill. She made herself strong because no one else would be strong for her. She made herself independent because dependence had only ever led to disappointment.

But even in the depths of neglect, divine eyes never looked away. The world may have dismissed her, but God never did. "Can a mother forget the baby at her breast and have no compassion on the child she has borne? Though she may forget, I will not forget you." (Isaiah 49:15)

Years later, as she pieced together the fragments of her childhood, she realized she had never been truly unseen. Every tear shed in loneliness had been counted. Every silent ache had been heard. And though the neglect of man had wounded her, the love of God was rewriting her story.

Rejection had been her past, but restoration was becoming her future. "The Lord will restore the years the locusts have eaten." (Joel 2:25

6. SPIRITUAL ABUSE

The misuse of religious beliefs or spiritual authority to control, manipulate, or oppress someone.

It can include using faith to justify mistreatment, shame, or coercion.

In her desperate search for answers, Tanwa found herself drawn deeper into the world of faith, seeking solace in the presence of religious people. Many were a beacon of hope—offering inspiration, support, and encouragement. And through it all, her gift of singing became a key, unlocking doors, she never imagined possible.

But just when it seemed like she was on the right path, she crossed paths with Abigail. A woman draped in spiritual authority yet lost in her own turmoil. Abigail was searching too—longing for purpose, wrestling with shadows she refused to name. Yet beneath her outward devotion lay a hidden struggle, an addiction that had long chained her to secrecy.

Abigail took an interest in Tanwa, drawn to her innocence and her hunger for truth. But what should have been mentorship became manipulation. Twisting Scripture to fit her desires, Abigail wove a distorted gospel—one that almost pulled Tanwa into a darkness she wasn't meant to know.

But just as she teetered on the edge of deception, God intervened. His hand, ever steady, pulled her away from the brink. "Your ears shall hear a word behind you, saying, 'This is the way, walk in it,' whenever you turn to the right hand or whenever you turn to the left." (Isaiah 30:21)

It was another near miss. Yet another reminder that even when the enemy disguises himself as light, God's love never lets go. He had seen her wandering, and once again, He had shown up—just in time.

7. DIGITAL/TECHNOLOGICAL ABUSE

This involves using technology to harass, stalk, manipulate, or control someone.

Some famous examples include cyberbullying, monitoring social media, sharing private information without consent, or using tracking devices.

In her quest for vulnerability, Tanwa took a bold step—she began sharing her story on social media. With trembling fingers, she peeled back the layers of her past, hoping that honesty would bring healing. However, instead of compassion, the first wave that hit her was criticism.

"Why did you attract so much drama?"

"What part of this was your fault?"

The words cut deep, reopening wounds she thought had begun to heal. The world, it seemed, was far more comfortable with silence than with truth. Fear crept in, and for a while, she retreated, questioning whether her voice was worth the backlash.

But then, something incredible happened. In the midst of the noise, a different sound emerged—the voices of others who had also suffered in silence. One by one, they reached out, sharing their buried pains and their hidden scars.

Tanwa realised then that her story wasn't just hers—it was a bridge, a light guiding others toward their healing. And as they walked that path together, the power of shared pain turned into the power of shared healing.

"They overcame him by the blood of the Lamb and by the word of their testimony." (Revelation 12:11)

Her voice, once trembling, became unshakable—because she had learned that the very thing meant to silence her was the very thing that set her free.

8. INSTITUTIONAL ABUSE

This kind of abuse is restricted to an environment. Usually, it occurs in organisations like schools, churches, nursing homes, or workplaces where individuals in power mistreat others.

It can involve neglect, exploitation, or systematic mistreatment of vulnerable individuals.

Each type of abuse can have lasting effects, but healing is possible with awareness, support, and proper intervention. If you or someone you know is experiencing abuse, seeking help from a trusted person or professional can be a crucial first step.

When Tanwa stepped into university, she carried a dream—a vision of studying a course she was passionate about, one that would shape her future. For a moment, it seemed like life had finally aligned in her favour. But fate, once again, had other plans.

One of the main lecturers in her department had a reputation—a silent predator lurking behind his position of power. He wielded influence not through wisdom but through coercion, ensuring that no pretty girl passed her exams unless she first surrendered to his desires.

Tanwa recognised the danger early. The lingering glances, the veiled suggestions—it was a game she had seen before—but she refused to play. However, refusing came at a cost. Instead of fighting a battle that felt rigged from the start, she walked away, abandoning the course she had once dreamed of.

Forced to pivot, she found herself on an entirely different academic path, one she hadn't planned for, one that felt like yet another stolen choice. But even in the detour, purpose awaited her. "Many are the plans in a person's heart, but it is the Lord's purpose that prevails." (Proverbs 19:21)

What seemed like a setback was in reality a redirection. And though she didn't know it yet, the course she never intended to take would lead her exactly where she was meant to be.

Healing from abuse is incredibly complex because, in most situations, it involves deep betrayal, broken trust, and often, long-lasting emotional scars. Regardless, of its challenging path, healing is possible.

HEALING CHAPTER

Healing: Healing can take many forms—physical, emotional, spiritual or even relational. It's a journey that requires patience, self-compassion, and sometimes the support of others.

At the age of eleven—she was young, innocent and oblivious to the darkness that existed in the world around her. Although beautiful, she was just beginning to show the early signs of womanhood. Still, she wasn't ready for the changes that came with it. She was shy and unsure and hid beneath oversized clothes, trying to delay the adulthood that was creeping in too soon.

Tanwa's innocence influenced her to trust people easily, never questioning their intentions. She couldn't see the hidden dangers or be knowledgeable enough to recognise the subtle signs of predatory behaviour—especially in the very place that was believed to be safe.

With a very protective father, even though she grew up among boys, she never had the chance to build courage. "The fear of Popsy is the beginning of wisdom," everyone would say, so it was best to shrink into the shadows, never daring to step beyond the unseen lines drawn.

Finding solace in the daily interactions at a military high school—a place to briefly escape into the crowd. Yet, even there, never truly free. Father had ensured that all eyes were lurking, ready to report any sign of irresponsibility. That constant surveillance created timidity, always aware of the invisible watchful presence that kept her life in check. Living not just in fear of consequences but also in the fear of never truly being unseen.

On an otherwise ordinary afternoon, Tanwa was picked up early from school for an eye check-up. It was supposed to be routine, nothing out of the ordinary. But instead of returning to class, she was driven home. The house was empty. The silence was deafening.

In that moment, innocence was shattered. A new reality began.

Father instructed her to go up to his room. She obeyed without question, unaware of what was to come. When he joined her upstairs, his tone was different—calm but unsettling. He said he needed to teach her some things about life and her body. She was too young to understand, too trusting to question. But in that moment, something inside her shifted, a quiet alarm she didn't yet know how to hear.

That day, he awakened a sensation in her that she never knew existed—a feeling she didn't understand, one she wasn't meant to experience at that age.

As he drew closer, her body tensed, confusion clouding her mind. Then suddenly, the sound of the doorbell rang, phew.... breaking the moment. He stopped and let her be. But the damage was already done.

Her eyes remained haunted by the image of his male organ, erected, a threat she couldn't comprehend. Her body shivered, trapped in a whirlwind of fear and confusion, unable to make sense of what had just happened.

This was the foundation of her brokenness and trauma —the moment that shattered something deep within her. She began to feel less than who she once was, as if a part of her had been stolen before she even understood its worth.

The violation became a relentless nightmare, a sinister ritual that wove itself into the fabric of Tanwa's childhood. In her innocence, she resisted as best as she could, but every protest was met with a cruel ultimatum. The warning was clear—silence or suffering. And so, whenever she made the simple missteps that all children do, she was forced to endure the unspeakable again. The alternative: A beating so merciless it left her body bleeding. In those moments, she had no real choice—only different shades of pain, each one stealing another piece of her soul.

She became withdrawn, locking away her emotions where no one could reach them. But in the midst of silence, she found solace in music. It became her refuge, the only thing that kept her sane. Through melodies and lyrics, she found an escape route to express what she couldn't say and hold on to the fragments of herself that still remained.

Years dragged by in the shadows of her torment, but eventually, she completed high school and seized the first chance to escape. With nothing but the weight of her past pressing against her, she fled the city, determined to put as much distance as possible between herself and the man who had stolen her innocence. She avoided him like a curse, as though proximity alone could shackle her to the nightmares she so desperately wanted to leave behind.

At just 19, Tanwa ran—not for freedom's sake, but for *survival*.
Her father's house was no home; it was a silent prison where words bruised, love was locked away, and control wore the face of care. So she fled, clutching the fragments of her innocence,

desperate for air, for space, for *something different.*

She found herself in college—but more importantly, she found herself in the *house of God.*
Not the stained-glass kind, but the kind where broken hearts gathered, and worship pierced the ceilings. It was there, in that sacred space between escape and destiny, that she met **Yusuf**.

Yusuf wasn't just a student. He was a firebrand. Older by a few years, but lightyears ahead in spirit. He was the kind of believer who didn't just *talk* about God—he *carried* Him. He spoke in tongues like heaven was on his tongue, wrote songs as if the wind whispered lyrics into his soul, and dared to hand the microphone to misfits like Tanwa—young, unsure, still shedding the chains of her past.

He was admired—oh, every girl noticed him. But Yusuf was *different.*
Noble. Gentle. Unshakably focused.
And Tanwa, cautious and bruised by history, kept her distance. Yet Yusuf never crossed the

line. He didn't exploit her naivety—he *covered* it.
He didn't pursue her emotionally—he pursued her spiritually.
He pushed her to hunger for more of God.
He wasn't the answer—but he pointed her to *The Answer*.

That season rewrote Tanwa's story.
She started writing songs—songs that poured from wounds turned into wells.
She led worship—not just with her voice, but with a power she couldn't explain.
She stood in places of deliverance, raising hands once too heavy to lift.
She smiled again—not a practiced smile, but one rooted in a joy that defied logic.
It was the kind of joy only God could give.

Her prison had become her platform.
Her scars, now sacred stories.
And it all started when one man chose to reflect God's love rather than take advantage of her vulnerability.

Timothy 2:22

"Flee the evil desires of youth and pursue righteousness, faith, love and peace, along with those who call on the Lord out of a pure heart."
—Yusuf embodied this, and this led Tanwa into a pursuit of purity and deeper purpose.

Proverbs 27:17

"As iron sharpens iron, so one person sharpens another."
—Yusuf sharpened her both musically and spiritually.

Isaiah 61:3

"...to bestow on them a crown of beauty instead of ashes, the oil of joy instead of mourning, and a garment of praise instead of a spirit of despair."
—Tanwa's joy, songs, and smile were evidence of this divine exchange.

Romans 12:2

"Do not conform to the pattern of this world, but be transformed by the renewing of your mind..."

—Her mind was renewed in worship and spiritual growth, reshaping her identity.

In her quest for closure, Tanwa confronted her father multiple times, seeking answers and perhaps a semblance of peace. Each attempt was met with cold indifference; his arrogance remained unshaken, devoid of remorse or regret. It was as if, given the chance, he would repeat his actions without hesitation.

Each time Tanwa's eyes met her mother's, her heart splintered into a thousand shards—each fragment echoing the raw, trembling vulnerability and paralysing dread that had long chained her mother to a life of silent suffering, a life ruled by a tyrant whose relentless wrongs left scars too deep to ever fully heal.

It took a very long time—decades, in fact—to finally confront her fears and begin to heal from this traumatic experience. For years, she carried the weight of that brokenness, letting it shape how she saw herself and the world around her.

But through it all, God never let go. Slowly, she found the strength to step out of the shadows, to reclaim her voice, and to tap back into the destiny Her Heavenly Father had planned for her. It wasn't easy; grace carried her through. And now, she stands not as a victim but as a testimony of healing, redemption, and purpose.

Healing from trauma or abuse is a deeply personal and often challenging journey, but it is possible. It takes time, support, and self-compassion. Here are some key steps that can help in the process:

1. Acknowledge and Accept Your Experience

Recognising what happened and allowing yourself to validate your pain is crucial. Suppressing or minimising it can delay healing.

Many survivors struggle with denial or self-blame, especially when the abuser is a parent or a trusted relative or friend. Recognising that what happened was wrong and not your fault is a crucial step toward healing.

2. Seek Safe Support

Surround yourself with people who uplift and support you—trusted friends, family, church, or a counsellor who specialises in trauma recovery.

Survivors often carry their pain in silence, fearing judgment or disbelief. Finding a safe space—whether with trusted friends, a therapist, a support group, or faith-based counselling—can provide much-needed validation and strength.

A trained counsellor or therapist can help process trauma in a safe way and offer strategies for overcoming its effects.

3. Allow Yourself to Feel and Express Emotions

It's okay to feel anger, sadness, grief, or confusion. Writing, speaking to a therapist, or engaging in creative expression like music or art can be therapeutic.

Therapy, especially trauma-informed counselling can help in processing painful memories and breaking free from emotional triggers.

Journaling, art, and music can also be powerful outlets.

4. Challenge Negative Beliefs

Abuse often leaves deep emotional scars, including feelings of unworthiness or self-blame. Replacing those lies with truth is an important step toward healing.

5. Rebuilding Self-Worth

Abuse often leaves survivors feeling ashamed or unworthy. Reconnecting with your values — through self-care, positive affirmations, or even service to others—helps reclaim your identity beyond the trauma.

Rebuilding self-worth must be a conscious act—a challenging journey, especially if self-esteem has been diminished for a long period. One effective approach is to immerse oneself in self-care readings and embrace practical efforts, even when they push you out of your comfort zone. In the process, you may find that some people drift away, struggling to accept your newfound outlook. However, those who remain will eventually grow accustomed to and support your transformation.

6. Develop Healthy Coping Mechanisms

Engaging in activities that bring you peace—prayer, journaling, exercise, singing, or being in nature—can help rebuild your sense of self.

7. Setting Boundaries

Creating firm boundaries (or cutting ties if necessary) is an important part of protecting your well-being. You have every right to distance yourself from anything that threatens your peace.

Setting boundaries became a critical turning point in her journey toward healing and self-respect. She discovered that by clearly defining what was acceptable and what was not, she could protect herself from further exploitation and reclaim control over her life. With time and courage, she began asserting her needs and enforcing her personal space—an act that was both empowering and necessary. Though the process was challenging and sometimes meant distancing herself from those unwilling to respect her limits, it ultimately laid the foundation for healthier relationships and a renewed sense of self-worth.

8. Finding Purpose Beyond the Pain

Many survivors use their experiences to help others, whether through advocacy, counselling, art, or simply being a source of encouragement. Your healing story has power — it can be a light for someone still in the darkness.

Surviving that kind of pain — especially when it's compounded by further betrayal — can make it feel easier to push everything down and keep going. Sometimes, survival mode is the only way to cope.

But true healing isn't just about being strong enough to endure; it's about allowing yourself to release the weight you've been carrying. Denial, misplaced trust, and avoidance are all part of the journey — many survivors go through similar cycles before they realise that healing has to come from within, on their own terms.

Resilience is powerful, but real freedom comes when you no longer have to hold everything inside.

Yes, healing is an everyday journey—a process, not a destination. It's not about waking up one day completely free of pain, but about choosing, day by day, to move forward in your own way.

9. Explore Forgiveness for Your Own Healing (If and When You're Ready)

Forgiveness is deeply personal—it doesn't mean excusing the abuse but rather releasing yourself from the hold of resentment and pain. It's a personal decision that happens in its own time. It's okay if you're not there yet; healing happens in layers.

Forgiveness is one of the hardest steps in the healing journey, yet the freedom it brings is beyond measure.

Unforgiveness keeps you trapped in the cage of your predator, binding you to the pain they inflicted. But choosing to forgive—whether or not they ask for it—is not for them; it's for you. It's about releasing yourself from their hold, breaking free from the weight of resentment.

Tanwa made the bold choice to forgive her father—not because he sought it, but for the freedom of her own soul. Yet, she guarded her heart, keeping firm boundaries in their relationship. Then, just before his final breath, the words she never expected but always deserved escaped his lips—an apology. And with that, the last piece of her healing fell into place.

However, forgiveness does not mean allowing them to continue invading your boundaries. Forgive, but don't forget. Heal, but stay wise. Let go, but never lose yourself again.

10. Rebuild Your Identity and Purpose

Abuse can strip away self-worth. Yet, it's essential to rediscover who you are beyond the pain and lean into your passions and purpose.

Healing is not linear, and there will be good and bad days. But with time, faith, and the right support, wholeness is possible. You're not alone, and your healing matters.

What Everyday Healing Can Look Like:

1. Allowing Yourself to Feel – Some days will be harder than others. Instead of suppressing emotions, acknowledge them with kindness. Healing isn't about "getting over it" but learning to navigate the emotions when they surface.

2. Rewriting Your Narrative – Abuse does not define you. Every day, you have the chance to remind yourself that, "I am more than what happened to me. I am whole, worthy, and free."

3. Practicing Self-Compassion – Be gentle with yourself. Healing takes time, and setbacks don't mean you're failing. They're just part of the process.

In the thick fog of depression, with wounds still raw from life's relentless blows—especially the fresh sting of a bitter divorce—Tanwa stood at a crossroads. Though her soul was weary, a fire still flickered within her. She longed to transform her pain into purpose, to become a light for others lost in the same darkness she had known.

So, she opened her arms. She opened her heart. She opened her life to Banke—a single mother of two, carrying not just the weight of motherhood but also the pain of a physical disability. Tanwa saw her, really saw her, and something in her spirit responded. Compassion overflowed. She brought Banke into her home, embraced her children like her own, and offered a safe haven wrapped in love and hope. She believed that healing could be contagious… that broken could find broken and together rise whole.

But what she received in return was betrayal cloaked in familiarity.

Banke mistook kindness for weakness and saw Tanwa's vulnerability not as a gift—but as an opportunity. With cold intent, she struck. She poisoned trust, sabotaged sacred bonds, and with venom in her voice, looked Tanwa in the eyes and vowed to destroy everything she had built—her ministry, her home, her relationships.

The betrayal was sharp. But instead of breaking Tanwa, it bent her toward a deeper intimacy with God. She realised that the enemy doesn't always come with a snarl—sometimes, he comes cloaked in need. She tightened her grip on the Word, guarding her heart with divine wisdom, learning that not everyone who knocks should be welcomed in.

This was no longer just survival. It was warfare.

And Tanwa learned to fight not just with kindness, but with discernment.

Proverbs 4:23
"Above all else, guard your heart, for everything you do flows from it."
—Tanwa learned to protect the wellspring of her life.

Proverbs 13:20
"Walk with the wise and become wise, for a companion of fools suffers harm."
—A reminder that who we walk with affects our destiny.

Matthew 7:6
"Do not give dogs what is sacred; do not throw your pearls to pigs. If you do, they may trample them under their feet, and turn and tear you to pieces."
—Even Jesus warned about offering precious things to those who won't value them.

Proverbs 27:6
"Wounds from a friend can be trusted, but an enemy multiplies kisses."

—Not everyone close is a friend; some only pretend to care.

1 Corinthians 15:33
"Do not be misled: 'Bad company corrupts good character.'"
—Tanwa's story is a testament to how proximity to the wrong spirit can be damaging.

Psalm 1:1
"Blessed is the one who does not walk in step with the wicked or stand in the way that sinners take..."
—True blessing begins with wise alignment.

4. Building Healthy Connections – Surrounding yourself with safe, uplifting people who see and support you can make the journey lighter.

5. Reclaiming Your Body and Mind – Reclaiming your body and mind is an essential approach to healing. Through prayer, meditation on God's Word, exercise, music, journal-

ing, or therapy—whatever helps you feel in control and at peace.

6. Letting Go in Layers – Healing doesn't mean forgetting, but it does mean loosening the grip the past has on you. Each day, you release a little more at your own pace.

7. Finding Purpose in Your Pain – Whether it's through helping others, creating, or simply living in joy, your journey can inspire and bring hope.

Healing is an act of courage, and you're already living it.

There is deep healing in sharing. Speaking your truth—whether through words, music, writing, or even quiet conversations with trusted people—can lift the weight of silence and shame.

How Sharing Your Story Brings Healing:

1. Breaking the Silence – Abuse thrives in secrecy, but sharing your story reclaims your power. You are no longer controlled by what happened; you are owning your narrative.

2. Validation and Release – When you share, especially with safe people, you receive acknowledgment and understanding. It confirms that what you went through matters and that you are seen and heard.

3. Connecting with Others – Your story can help others who are still struggling in silence. It can give them hope, showing them that healing is possible.

4. Reframing the Narrative – Speaking about your experience helps separate you from it. You're not just a survivor; you are a whole person with strength, resilience, and a future beyond the past.

5. Letting Go of Shame – Sharing removes the illusion that you have something to hide. You did nothing wrong. The more you speak, the more the shame loses its grip.

6. Owning Your Power – Every time you tell your story; you take control of it. It's no longer just about what happened to you—it's about what you're doing with it.

7. Creating Purpose from Pain – Whether you share one-on-one or with a wider audience, your experience can be a source of encouragement, advocacy, or ministry to others.

SELF ESTEEM CHAPTER

Self-esteem is the way we perceive and value ourselves. It reflects our overall sense of self-worth, confidence, and belief in our abilities. Healthy self-esteem means recognising our strengths, accepting our imperfections and believing that we are worthy of love, respect and success.

There are two main types of self-esteem:

1.   High self-esteem – A positive self-view, confidence in one's abilities and resilience in facing challenges.

2.   Low self-esteem – Feelings of self-doubt, worthlessness or insecurity, often influenced by past experiences, criticism, or trauma.

Self-esteem is not fixed—it can grow, and change based on experiences, mind-set, and intentional self-care.

Healing from abuse can take a toll on self-esteem, but rebuilding it is part of the journey. Self-esteem isn't just about confidence—it's about knowing your worth, believing in yourself, and treating yourself with love and respect.

Ways to Rebuild Self-Esteem After Abuse:

1. Challenge Negative Thoughts

Abuse often plants lies like "I'm not enough" or "I don't deserve good things." Replace those with truth: "I am worthy, I am loved, I am strong.

2. Practice Self-Compassion

Speak to yourself the way you'd speak to a dear friend. Healing takes time, and you deserve patience and kindness from yourself.

3. Surround Yourself with Positivity

Be intentional about the people, music, books, and environments that affirm your worth instead of tearing you down.

Surrounding yourself with the right people—those who radiate love, faith, and light—is crucial on the journey of healing from trauma. Tanwa was divinely surrounded by such souls. She was graced with an extraordinary circle—beautiful hearts who held her emotionally, stood with her physically, lifted her in prayer, and even supported her financially. Their love became an invisible anchor, keeping her grounded in ways they may never fully understand. Her radiant smile and joyful countenance were often a reflection of just how richly blessed she was.

She had an adopted mum and dad who became pillars in her life—standing in the gap when her strength waned. They walked with her through the sacred yet vulnerable moments of childbirth, especially when she was wheeled into the theatre to bring her daughter into the world. In her darkest hours—grieving the loss of her biological mother—they didn't hesitate to drive across towns in the middle of the night just to hold her, to open their home and hearts when hers felt shattered.

Whenever Tanwa's world shattered into pieces, when the silence of pain grew too loud to bear, it was her adopted parents she turned to—her refuge, her lifeline. In their embrace, she found more than comfort; she found healing. They weren't just guardians of her journey—they were God's chosen vessels, tenderly mending the fractures of her soul. And in the seasons where she bloomed, radiant and rising, it was their unwavering love that had watered her roots. Through every storm and sunrise, they stood—anointed instruments of divine restoration, her sacred place of both breaking and becoming.

Psalm 68:6
"God sets the lonely in families, he leads out the prisoners with singing…"

Isaiah 61:1-3
"…He has sent me to bind up the brokenhearted, to proclaim freedom for the captives… to comfort all who mourn… to bestow on them a crown of beauty instead of ashes.

Romans 8:28

"And we know that in all things God works for the good of those who love him, who have been called according to his purpose."

Her journey was also shielded by the loving arms of spiritual brothers and sisters who showed up when she needed it most. During her caesarean surgeries, they didn't just wait—they waged war in the spirit. Pacing the hospital hallway, they turned it into holy ground, lifting fervent prayers, interceding with every step, contending for her life. While surgeons worked inside, they partnered with Heaven outside, standing in the gap with unwavering faith — bringing flowers, meals, comforting hugs, and gentle smiles that spoke louder than words. Among them was her dear church sister Roseline, whose selfless love for Tanwa and her children mirrored the very heart of Christ.

The church became more than a building—it was the home of her Father, the sanctuary where her soul found rest. Her bond with her church family and fellow music ministers was unbreakable. In them, she found not just community, but a sacred tribe that breathed strength into her journey. It was a gift she would forever hold close to her heart.

John 16:33

"I have told you these things, so that in me you may have peace. In this world you will have trouble. But take heart! I have overcome the world."
—Jesus Himself reminds us that trials are part of the journey, but His victory is our assurance.

Isaiah 43:2

"When you pass through the waters, I will be with you; and when you pass through the rivers, they will not sweep over you. When you walk through the fire, you will not be burned…"
—Not a promise of an easy road, but of divine presence and protection through it all.

Romans 8:18

"I consider that our present sufferings are not worth comparing with the glory that will be revealed in us."

—A reminder that the hard road has a purpose—glory awaits on the other side.

2 Corinthians 4:8-9

"We are hard pressed on every side, but not crushed; perplexed, but not in despair; persecuted, but not abandoned; struck down, but not destroyed."

—Even when the journey feels unbearable, God's sustaining power keeps us.

Matthew 7:13-14

"Enter through the narrow gate. For wide is the gate and broad is the road that leads to destruction... But small is the gate and narrow the road that leads to life, and only a few find it."

—The right path is often the hardest, but it leads to life.

4. Reclaim Your Power

Set boundaries. Say no. Take up space. Make choices that honour your well-being. These are all acts of self-respect.

5. Celebrate Small Wins

Every step forward matters. Whether it's speaking up, prioritising your needs or simply getting through a tough day—acknowledge your progress.

6. Engage in What Brings You Joy

Music, dance, prayer, journaling, fitness—anything that reconnects you to your true self beyond the pain.

Tanwa was undeniably marked by divine favour.
Not the kind you could explain… but the kind that left even *her* in awe.

Doors opened where there were no hallways.
Opportunities came that left others wondering, *"Why her?"* And truth be told, Tanwa often asked the same question. She knew—deep in the quiet of her soul—that she hadn't *earned this*. This was grace. Pure, unfiltered grace. The kind that chooses you when you feel most unworthy.

Then came the moment that turned everything.
At one of her lowest points, when life felt like an echo chamber of disappointment, she crossed paths with Jonathan—a meeting so casual, it could've gone unnoticed. But heaven was orchestrating something. Jonathan, prompted by a simple comment from a mutual friend, noticed her voice... her gift. A gift she had almost silenced under the weight of life.

Jonathan wasn't just anyone. He was the host of a renowned international TV program. And in what felt like a dream, he offered Tanwa a spot-on national television. Suddenly, the girl who had once questioned her relevance was being seen, celebrated, *known*.

Lights. Cameras. Worship.
Tanwa stepped onto that platform not just as a singer, but as a testimony. Clothed in her best garments—her princess moments—she stood radiant. With every note she sang, hearts were stirred, chains broke, and lives were touched. Her gift became a river, flowing from her pain, spilling into purpose.

Crowds cheered. Friends rejoiced. Family wept in pride.

And Tanwa? She smiled.

Not with arrogance, but with *hope*. A quiet, confident knowing that her tomorrow was *indeed bright*. That even when life had buried her, God had always planned to resurrect her.

Samuel 2:8

"He raises the poor from the dust and lifts the needy from the ash heap; he seats them with princes and has them inherit a throne of honour."

—Tanwa's journey was a throne-from-the-ash-heap story.

Psalm 75:6-7

"For promotion cometh neither from the east, nor from the west, nor from the south. But God is the judge: he puts down one and sets up another."

—Her rise wasn't man-made. It was God-ordained.

Zechariah 4:6
"'Not by might nor by power, but by my Spirit,' says the Lord Almighty."
—It wasn't her doing. It was His Spirit opening every door.

Esther 2:17
"Now the king was attracted to Esther more than to any of the other women... So, he set a royal crown on her head..."
—Like Esther, Tanwa walked into favour that crowned her.

Matthew 5:14-16
"You are the light of the world... let your light shine before others, that they may see your good deeds and glorify your Father in heaven."
—Her gift wasn't just for fame. It was to glorify the One who lit her flame.

7. Affirm Your Identity Beyond the Past

You are not just what you've been through. You are gifted, strong, valuable, and full of purpose.

WAITING CHAPTER

Waiting can be one of the most challenging experiences, especially when you're waiting for something that feels significant or uncertain. It can bring up feelings of impatience, frustration, or even anxiety. But waiting can also teach us patience, resilience, and trust in timing—whether it's waiting for healing, a change in circumstances, or a breakthrough.

Waiting for something as profound as the fruit of the womb was emotionally and physically draining for her, and seven years of waiting is a testament to her strength, faith, and resilience. During such a long wait, there's often a mix of hope, heartache, and sometimes doubt.

The loneliness and withdrawal that came with such a long waiting period were deeply painful. When we're in the space of waiting for something so meaningful, it can feel isolating—like others might not fully understand the depth of our experience, and she even began to question if it will ever happen.

Tanwa's heart ached with every month that passed. The empty womb felt like an echo chamber of shame and longing. She had prayed, fasted, cried — but still, no baby. So, she turned to the one place everyone said held answers: the hospital. Science, they told her, would do what time and faith had not yet done.

She walked into those clinics with trembling hope — hope that maybe this time, her story would change. That maybe the cold tools and white coats would finally bring the miracle she'd bled for in silence.

But what awaited her there wasn't healing — it was horror dressed as help.

Behind closed doors, certain doctors saw not a woman in need, but a woman they believed they could manipulate. A woman desperate enough to keep silent. They tried to take advantage of her vulnerability — with their twisted promises and unclean hands. One told her,

"You'll never carry life unless you let me make it happen." Another whispered lie cloaked in medical jargon, touching her in ways no procedure required.

They made her feel like her womb was a bargaining chip.

They tried to convince her that *they* were the key — that her miracle was tied to their perversion. That without their involvement, her barrenness would be permanent. It wasn't medicine they were offering — it was manipulation wrapped in a white coat.

And yet, Tanwa did not break.

Though shaken, she refused to surrender the last piece of herself. She began to see through the performance — the charm that masked corruption. And even though it cost her tears, delays, and another layer of trauma, she walked away. Empty womb and all — but with her soul still intact.

Because she finally realized: *No one holds the power to her miracle but God.*

In Vitro Fertilisation (IVF) can be an emotional rollercoaster, and getting pregnant in the process after waiting for so long must have been both overwhelming and joyous. It's a testament to her resilience and the strength she found through the process, even when things felt difficult.

After such a long wait, it felt almost too surreal to be true.

Buying baby clothes, preparing a space, and taking those tangible steps were a way of bridging the gap between disbelief and joy. It was almost like creating physical markers that make the dream feel real and give something to look forward to.

When we go through a period of waiting and longing, the reality of what we've been hoping for can be hard to fully accept when it finally arrives.

The emotional weight of carrying the joy of pregnancy while experiencing the heartache of her mother's brain tumour was incredibly difficult. Grief and joy can coexist and navigating both can be overwhelming.

Feeling both the joy and the pain and yet being unable to fully share that with the people closest to you is overwhelming. Grief can make us feel isolated, and when combined with the physical and emotional intensity of pregnancy, it can leave you feeling even more withdrawn. Sometimes, even the people we love can struggle to understand the depth of what we're going through, especially when it's a mix of loss and new life.

The moment she finally met her baby was indescribable—after all the years of waiting, the heartache, and the struggles, the joy was a beautiful, healing experience. It was incredible how new life can bring a sense of peace and fulfilment, even after all the challenges leading up to it.

What a beautiful full circle—going from the long wait to the joy of being a mother of four. That journey feels even more meaningful now, knowing how much it took to get there. The joy of motherhood, especially after such a journey, feels all the more precious.

GRIEF CHAPTER

Losing her mum while navigating the joy of motherhood was an incredibly complex and bittersweet experience. The grief of losing a parent, especially when you're in the midst of nurturing a new life, can be a significant surge of mixed emotions.

That kind of grief can feel so raw, especially when you're not ready to say goodbye. It's understandable to wish things were different; you long for the presence of someone you love deeply. The pain of losing a mother, especially when you're going through something as transformative as motherhood, can feel like a huge void that's hard to fill.

Even though the pain still lingers, the love and bond she had with MoMo remain, and it's okay if she's still taking time to navigate that. Grief doesn't follow a set timeline—it's personal and unique.

It was heart-breaking to face another loss (marriage), especially when there's already so much emotional weight from everything else. Losing a marriage can feel like losing a part of yourself, and the grief that comes with that can be just as complex as any other form of loss.

Betrayal, heartbreak, and low self-esteem shone through the façade of her forced smile—a smile that everyone around her could see—one that betrayed the deep pain hidden beneath its surface.

Overcoming grief was an arduous journey for Tanwa, yet she understood that the first step was to acknowledge her pain. By extricating herself from the environment that had long nurtured her sorrow and clinging to the hope of a brighter tomorrow, she began to forge a path toward healing.

With everything she already navigated—the waiting for her children, the grief of losing her mom—this must feel like another layer of deep pain. The mix of emotions that comes with the end of a marriage can include anger, sadness, confusion, and sometimes even guilt, especially when it feels like a chapter of your life is closing.

Losing her marriage and home while navigating the challenges of single motherhood can feel overwhelming, especially after all the grief she already faced.

The hurt from the breakdown of a marriage can be cut so deeply, especially when it's something you invested so much of your heart and hope into. It's not just the loss of a relationship but the loss of shared dreams, trust, and the vision of what you thought your future would be. The pain from this can be overwhelming, and it's completely understandable that it would leave a mark.

Leaving everything behind and moving cities to start afresh in a completely new environment during the intensity of the lockdown, especially with kids, took so much courage and determination. The unknown can be both thrilling and terrifying, but the fact that she chose to move forward for her family, and her future is a powerful testament to her resilience.

Rejection, especially after everything she's already been through, felt like a deep wound. It's not just about the specific situation or person but the emotional toll it took on her sense of worth and belonging. Rejection can make us question ourselves, our values and our place in the world.

When rejection comes from those we care about or situations that feel out of our control, it can be especially painful.

Finding yourself after so much change, loss, and emotional strain is such an important and personal journey. It's about reconnecting with who you are, what you need, and what you want out of life moving forward. Sometimes, this journey of self-discovery can feel overwhelming, especially after so much has been out of your control. But finding yourself is a process of peeling back the layers—rediscovering your strengths, passions, and values and deciding that you need to feel whole again.

An intentional, happy life is such a powerful goal, especially after everything you've faced. It's about making choices that align with your values and well-being and not simply letting life happen to you. It's a commitment to finding joy in the small moments, setting boundaries that protect your peace, and creating a life that feels fulfilling and true to who you are.

Living intentionally means prioritising what truly matters to you—whether that's self-care, nurturing your relationships, pursuing your passions, or creating new experiences. It also means being kind to yourself through the hard days because joy doesn't always come in big, perfect moments; sometimes, it's found in the quiet, everyday things.

Risk-taking can be a powerful tool for growth and transformation, though it often comes with fear and uncertainty. After everything you've been through, embracing risks may feel both exciting and intimidating, but it's also a way of asserting control over your future and pushing yourself into new, sometimes uncomfortable, spaces where growth happens.

Taking risks could be anything from starting a new business, trusting people again, trying something new for your own happiness, or stepping outside your comfort zone in small ways. It's about knowing that even if the outcome isn't perfect, the act of taking a risk often leads to new lessons, opportunities, and self-discovery.

Turning passion into reality isn't always easy, but it's often the most rewarding. It takes courage to take that leap and trust in your ability to create something meaningful. That's such a brave and empowering step!

Taking on projects that feel beyond you can be intimidating, but it's also where growth and transformation happen. It's a way to stretch yourself, learn new skills, and prove to yourself that you're capable of more than you might have imagined. That feeling of stepping into something bigger than you can be is empowering, even when it comes with uncertainty and a bit of fear.

"Faith over fear" is such a powerful mindset, especially when you're taking on projects or risks that seem beyond your current capabilities. Choosing faith means trusting that you have the strength, wisdom, and resilience to navigate whatever challenges come your way. It's the belief that you're not alone in the process and that even in moments of doubt or fear, there's a greater purpose and plan guiding you.

Prioritising living with faith over fear doesn't mean you won't feel fear—it's natural. But it's about choosing to act in spite of it, knowing that you can face whatever comes next.

The word of God can provide a deep sense of peace, encouragement, and direction when things feel uncertain. It's often in those moments of fear or struggle that verses and promises can stand as anchors, reminding you of the greater plan and the strength available to you.

It's a powerful combination to believe you are made for more and grounding that belief in the word of God. It gives you a deep sense of purpose and conviction, knowing that there's a divine purpose in your life and that you have the strength to walk in it.

It's such a liberating truth to hold onto—the idea that your story, no matter how difficult, doesn't define your future. The word of God reminds us that we're not bound by our past or our struggles. Here are a few Bible verses that align with that powerful belief:

Isaiah 43:18-19

"Forget the former things; do not dwell on the past. See, I am doing a new thing! Now it springs up; do you not perceive it? I am making a way in the wilderness and streams in the wasteland."

This verse speaks to God's promise of new beginnings, no matter where you've come from.

2 Corinthians 5:17

"Therefore, if anyone is in Christ, the new creation has come: The old has gone, the new is here!"

This verse affirms that in Christ, you're made new. Your past doesn't define who you are today or where you're headed.

Romans 8:1

"Therefore, there is now no condemnation for those who are in Christ Jesus."

No matter what you've been through, this verse reminds you that you're not defined by your mistakes or struggles.

Jeremiah 29:11

For I know the plans I have for you," declares the Lord, "plans to prosper you and not to harm you, plans to give you a hope and a future."

God's plan for your life is greater than any chapter of hardship you've faced. You have a future filled with hope.

Philippians 3:13-14

"Brothers and sisters, I do not consider myself yet to have taken hold of it. But one thing I do: Forgetting what is behind and straining toward what is ahead, I press on toward the goal to win the prize for which God has called me heavenward in Christ Jesus."

This reminds us that, despite our past, we are pressing toward a future that God has called us to.

Perseverance is such an important theme in the Bible, and there are many scriptures that encourage us to keep going, even in the face of trials. Here are a few verses that speak to perseverance and the strength that comes from trusting in God through difficult times:

James 1:2-4

"Consider it pure joy, my brothers and sisters, whenever you face trials of many kinds, because you know that the testing of your faith produces perseverance. Let perseverance finish its work so that you may be mature and complete, not lacking anything."

This reminds us that trials are a part of the process, and that perseverance shapes our character and spiritual maturity.

Romans 5:3-4

"Not only so, but we also glory in our sufferings, because we know that suffering produces perseverance; perseverance, character; and character, hope."

Here, the Bible shows that perseverance is a key part of developing hope and character through suffering.

Galatians 6:9

"Let us not become weary in doing good, for at the proper time we will reap a harvest if we do not give up."

This verse encourages us to stay faithful in doing good, knowing that the reward comes to those who persevere.

Hebrews 12:1-2

"Therefore, since we are surrounded by such a great cloud of witnesses, let us throw off everything that hinders and the sin that so easily entangles. And let us run with perseverance the race marked out for us, fixing our eyes on Jesus, the pioneer and perfecter of faith."

This passage encourages us to keep our eyes on Jesus and persevere, no matter the challenges, because He is our ultimate example.

2 Timothy 4:7

"I have fought the good fight, I have finished the race, I have kept the faith."

Paul's words are a declaration of perseverance in faith, no matter the struggles faced along the way.

Isaiah 40:31

"But those who hope in the Lord will renew their strength. They will soar on wings like eagles; they will run and not grow weary; they will walk and not be faint."

This verse assures us that God's strength renews us when we persevere through challenges.

The Bible offers profound insights into why God allows us to experience pain and suffering, and many of these verses emphasise how pain can lead to growth, deeper faith, and a closer relationship with Him. Here are some scriptures that help us understand the purpose behind pain:

Romans 5:3-5

"Not only so, but we also glory in our sufferings because we know that suffering produces perseverance; perseverance, character; and character, hope. And hope does not put us to shame, because God's love has been poured out into our hearts through the Holy Spirit, who has been given to us."

This scripture reminds us that suffering isn't in vain; it produces perseverance, character, and hope, ultimately drawing us closer to God's love.

James 1:2-4

"Consider it pure joy, my brothers and sisters, whenever you face trials of many kinds, because you know that the testing of your faith produces perseverance. Let perseverance finish its work so that you may be mature and complete, not lacking anything."

Pain and trials are tests that lead to spiritual maturity and completeness in Christ, refining our faith and character.

2 Corinthians 1:3-4

"Praise be to the God and Father of our Lord Jesus Christ, the Father of compassion and the God of all comfort, who comforts us in all our troubles, so that we can comfort those in any trouble with the comfort we ourselves receive from God."

God allows pain so that we can experience His comfort and, in turn, share that comfort with others who are hurting. Our pain becomes a way to empathise with and help others.

Hebrews 12:11

"No discipline seems pleasant at the time, but painful. Later on, however, it produces a harvest of righteousness and peace for those who have been trained by it."

Pain can be a form of God's discipline, guiding us toward righteousness and peace. Although it is difficult momentarily, it has a lasting, positive effect on our spiritual growth.

1 Peter 1:6-7

"In all this you greatly rejoice, though now for a little while you may have had to suffer grief in all kinds of trials. These have come so that the proven genuineness of your faith—of greater worth than gold, which perishes even though refined by fire—may result in praise, glory, and honour when Jesus Christ is revealed."

Pain and suffering refine our faith, making it more genuine and valuable, much like gold being purified by fire.

2 Corinthians 4:17

"For our light and momentary troubles are achieving for us an eternal glory that far outweighs them all."

This verse encourages us to look beyond our current pain, knowing that the suffering we experience now is preparing us for something far greater in eternity.

Romans 8:18

"I consider that our present sufferings are not worth comparing with the glory that will be revealed in us."

This verse reminds us that the pain we endure in this life pales in comparison to the glory God has prepared for us, offering hope for the future.

Isaiah 55:8-9

"For my thoughts are not your thoughts, neither are your ways my ways," declares the Lord. *"As the heavens are higher than the

earth, so are my ways higher than your ways and my thoughts than your thoughts."

This reminds us that we may not always understand the reasons behind our pain, but God's wisdom and plan are far beyond our understanding.

These scriptures help us see that pain has a deeper purpose in God's plan for us. It can lead to growth, comfort, and even the ability to help others.

DON'T BLAME YOU CHAPTER

We all have a tendency to carry some weight on our hearts. Whatever it is, give yourself grace. You're human, and you're learning.

Just as you extend kindness and understanding to others, you deserve the same for yourself. Growth takes time, and mistakes don't define you—they shape you. Keep moving forward with love and patience for yourself.

Mistakes are a part of life, learning, and growth. What matters is how you rise from them, what you learn, and how you move forward. Be kind to yourself—you're still becoming.

It is important to encourage self-love, self-worth, and seeing yourself through God's eyes:

Mark 12:31

"The second is this: 'Love your neighbour as yourself.' There is no commandment greater than these."

This reminds us that loving ourselves is essential to loving others.

Psalm 139:14

"I praise you because I am fearfully and wonderfully made; your works are wonderful; I know that full well."

You are God's masterpiece, created with purpose and beauty.

Ephesians 2:10

"For we are God's handiwork, created in Christ Jesus to do good works, which God prepared in advance for us to do."

You are valuable because God created you with intention.

1 Corinthians 6:19-20

"Do you not know that your bodies are temples of the Holy Spirit, who is in you, whom you have received from God? You are not your own; you were bought at a price. Therefore, honour God with your bodies."

Taking care of yourself—physically, emotionally, and spiritually—is a way to honour God.

Romans 8:37-39

"No, in all these things we are more than conquerors through him who loved us. For I am convinced that neither death nor life, neither angels nor demons, neither the present nor the future, nor any powers, neither height nor depth, nor anything else in all creation, will be able to separate us from the love of God that is in Christ Jesus our Lord."

No matter what happens, God's love for you is unshakable!

Isaiah 43:4

"Since you are precious and honoured in my sight, and because I love you, I will give people in exchange for you, nations in exchange for your life."

God calls you precious and honoured. Believe in your worth.

Proverbs 19:8

"The one who gets wisdom loves life; the one who cherishes understanding will soon prosper."

Loving yourself includes seeking wisdom and valuing your own well-being.

Loving yourself isn't about pride or selfishness—it's about seeing yourself the way God does and living in that truth. You are loved, worthy, and made for more…Yes you are!

Life brings challenges, but not everything that happens is your fault. Sometimes, things are beyond your control, and blaming yourself only weighs you down. Instead of guilt, choose growth. Instead of regret, choose grace. God is always working things out for your good, even when you don't understand it.

Romans 8:28

"And we know that in all things God works for the good of those who love him, who have been called according to his purpose."

Sometimes, the biggest battles we fight are within ourselves—self-doubt, guilt, fear, or negative self-talk. But you don't have to be your own worst enemy.

God didn't create you to live in constant self-criticism. He calls you loved, chosen, and worthy. Instead of tearing yourself down, speak life over yourself.

2 Corinthians 10:5

"We demolish arguments and every pretension that sets itself up against the knowledge of God, and we take captive every thought to make it obedient to Christ."

Shift your mindset. Replace self-doubt with faith, fear with courage, and guilt with grace. You are not your enemy—you are God's masterpiece, a work in progress, growing into all He has called you to be.

Here are some positive declarations to speak over yourself instead of self-destruction:

I am loved and worthy.

"I am fearfully and wonderfully made" (Psalm 139:14). God created me with purpose, and I am valuable just as I am.

I am not my past mistakes.

"If anyone is in Christ, the new creation has come: The old has gone, the new is here!" (2 Corinthians 5:17). My past does not define me — God's grace does.

I choose faith over fear.

"For God has not given us a spirit of fear, but of power, love, and a sound mind" (2 Timothy 1:7). I walk boldly, knowing God is with me.

I forgive myself and move forward.

"There is now no condemnation for those who are in Christ Jesus" (Romans 8:1). I release guilt and embrace the new mercies God gives me daily.

I am strong and courageous.

"Be strong and courageous. Do not be afraid or discouraged, for the Lord your God is with you" (Joshua 1:9). No matter what I face, I will overcome.

I speak life over myself.

"The tongue has the power of life and death" (Proverbs 18:21). I choose to speak words of hope, strength, and faith over my life.

I am made for more.

"For I know the plans I have for you, declares the Lord, plans to prosper you and not to harm you, plans to give you hope and a future" (Jeremiah 29:11). My life has meaning and purpose.

You are not meant for self-destruction—you are meant for greatness, healing, and transformation. Keep declaring truth over your life!

STANDING IN LOVE CHAPTER

Opening your heart to love again after hurt and divorce is not easy, but it's possible with healing, faith, and self-love.

If you're reflecting on your experience, it will have to involve:

-Healing through God's love – Realising that His love never left you, even in the pain.

-Forgiveness – Not just for the past, but for yourself, which ultimately frees your heart from bitterness.

-Rebuilding self-worth – Understanding that you are still whole, still valuable, and still deserving of love.

-Trusting again – Learning to let go of fear and embrace new possibilities.

-Patience – Giving yourself time and grace to love at your own pace.

Standing in love means choosing to love with clarity, strength, and purpose rather than being swept away by fleeting emotions. It's about:

- Conscious commitment – Choosing love with wisdom, not just feelings.
- Emotional maturity – Loving from a place of wholeness, not desperation.
- Mutual respect – Building a foundation on trust, honesty, and shared values.
- God-centred love – Allowing faith to guide your relationships rather than emotions alone.

Love isn't meant to make you lose yourself—it should strengthen you, uplift you, and align with your purpose. When you stand in love, you build something that lasts, and you're intentional about it.

The circle you surround yourself with when in a relationship or marriage has a huge impact on your growth, peace, and the success of that relationship. The right people will nurture, support, and guide you, while the wrong circle can sow doubt, confusion, and negativity.

Why the Right Circle Matters in your growth as you stand in love:

-Wise Counsel and Godly Influence

"Walk with the wise and become wise, for a companion of fools suffers harm." (Proverbs 13:20)

-Surround yourself with people who uplift your relationship and give godly advice, not those who encourage toxic behaviour or disrespect.

Encouragement, Not Comparison!

A strong circle reminds you that every relationship is unique. They celebrate your wins and guide you through struggles rather than making you feel less—because of someone else's journey.

-Accountability and Support

A good circle will challenge you to honour God in your relationship, hold you accountable, and pray with you instead of leading you into temptation or unhealthy patterns.

-Peace Over Drama

The right people protect your relationship, while the wrong crowd stirs unnecessary drama. Avoid circles that thrive on gossip or negativity about love and marriage.

-Healthy Individual Growth

Your circle should push you toward your purpose and growth in faith, wisdom, and emotional well-being. A strong relationship is built by two whole individuals—not by people who are only defined by their relationship.

How to Choose the Right Circle:

✔ Surround yourself with friends who support your values

✔ Seek mentors or couples who have wisdom and experience

✔ Distance yourself from toxic, negative, or envious influences

✔ Pray for discernment in choosing who speaks into your life.

A relationship is already a journey with its own challenges. The right circle protects, strengthens, and encourages it, while the wrong one can tear it down. Choose wisely!

A godly home is built on faith, love, and biblical principles, but that doesn't mean it's free from complexity. Challenges will come -differences in personalities, struggles in marriage, parenting hurdles, financial pressures and even spiritual battles. However, what makes a home truly godly is how these complexities are handled.

Keys to Navigating Complexity in a Godly Home:

1. **Christ as the Foundation**

"Unless the Lord builds the house, the builders labour in vain" (Psalm 127:1).

A home centred on God finds strength even in tough times.

2. Love and Grace in Difficult Times

"Above all, love each other deeply, because love covers a multitude of sins" (1 Peter 4:8).

A godly home thrives on forgiveness, patience and understanding.

3. Effective Communication

"Let your conversation be always full of grace, seasoned with salt" (Colossians 4:6).

Misunderstandings are natural, but grace-filled words bring healing, not division.

4. Spiritual Warfare and Prayer

"For our struggle is not against flesh and blood, but against the rulers, against the authorities, against the powers of this dark world" (Ephesians 6:12).

Challenges may be spiritual in nature. A praying home is a victorious home.

5. Raising Children in Faith Amid Modern Challenges

"Train up a child in the way he should go" (Proverbs 22:6).

The world's influence is strong, but intentional parenting grounded in biblical values makes a difference.

6. Resilience Through Trials

"Consider it pure joy, my brothers and sisters, whenever you face trials of many kinds" (James 1:2).

Complexity in a home is not a sign of failure—it's an opportunity for growth, refining, and deeper reliance on God.

A godly home doesn't mean a perfect home. It means a home where God's presence is welcomed, where love overcomes struggles and where faith holds everything together—even in challenging times.

CHANGED STORY CHAPTER

Strength is a testimony of resilience and healing, and God's grace is always at work in your life. Despite the pain, abuse and rejection, make sure you do not break— rather, Rise!

Your Strength is Proof That:

☑ God's grace is greater than your past. ("My grace is sufficient for you, for my power is made perfect in weakness." – 2 Corinthians 12:9)

☑ Pain didn't define you—it refined you.

☑ Rejection wasn't the end—it was a redirection to something greater.

☑ You are a walking proof of victory, not a victim of your past.

It is time to decree:

I am a warrior, and my story will end well. It will inspire many!

Keep standing, keep shining, keep fighting and keep believing—because you are made for more!

It's not over until it's over!